CREATE *Better* PAINTINGS

WORKING WITH PASTELS

ELSIE DI NARDO DRESCH

Copyright applied for July 20, 2006.

Elsie Di Nardo Dresch

3961 Sheldon Dr

Atlanta, Ga. 30342

Web Page www.elsiedresch.com

E-Mail elsiedresch@mindspring.com

ISBN-10: 0-9788524-0-0

"Morning Has Broken"
30" x 22"

DEDICATION

This book is dedicated to the loving memory of my son, Fred Dresch, who encouraged me from the beginning...

and to Janet and Jim Mozley, who supported me and cheered me on to the end.

ACKNOWLEDGEMENTS

To my students everywhere who kept me on my toes and enriched my life. Thank you.

To the many teachers who directed me along the path and let me choose my own way. Thank you.

To Barbara Fountain, my dear friend, who has been my sounding board, driver and assistant throughout the years. Thank you.

To Mark Windsor my computer guru who helped me work on my PC skills in preparing this book for print. Thank you.

To Bob Biedrzycki who altered my way of thinking and magically transformed my book, adding his unique flair. Thank you.

And to all my loving friends who helped make this book a reality. Thank you.

"Mountain Stream"
28" x 24"

ABOUT THE ARTIST ELSIE DI NARDO DRESCH

Energetic and enthusiastic, Elsie Dresch advises new students to do three things. First, join a local art group, so you will have friends and associates with the same interest and get support in your community. Second, subscribe to two art magazines of your choice, selecting one in the mediums in which you work, and one of general interest such as ART NEWS or AMERICAN ART REVIEW. Third, paint every day or do something directly related to art and painting, so that you get and remain focused on being serious about your work.

Elsie Dresch teaches workshops in North Carolina, Florida, and in Atlanta, Georgia where she has been living for many years.

Her art education began in Philadelphia at 13, when she studied at the Graphic Sketch Club, then attended the Fleisher Memorial School of Art. Her education continued in Baltimore with private instructions for six years and resumed in Atlanta, where she attended classes at the Atlanta College of Art, in addition to studying with several contemporary artists in workshops throughout the Southeast. She is a "Member of Excellence" of the Atlanta Artists Center and of the Southeastern Pastel Society, and a "Signature Member" of the Pastel Society of America. She has received over 60 awards in regional and national shows. Her work is in many private and corporate collections in United States, Canada and Italy.

She is represented in Atlanta by Watson Gallery, and Bobbe Gillis Inc., and in Blue Ridge, Georgia by High Country Arts and Antiques. In Beaufort, SC she has work at the I. Pinckney Simons Gallery.

INTRODUCTION

Pastel paintings are rich, brilliant, colorful and I love working with them. I am not alone because the popularity of the medium is increasing greatly. That's why I wrote Create Better Paintings (Working with Pastels), an instructional book that covers the What, Where and How of painting.

The book begins by providing you with some background: a description and a history of pastels. The information was supplied by the PASTEL SOCIETY OF AMERICA, the group largely responsible for the resurgence of pastels. You will also find a List of Materials and an explanation of Plein Air Painting vs. Studio Painting, describing the pros, cons and value of both methods. This is followed by step-by-step instructions on creating your own fabulous pastel painting.

You'll learn how to start your creation by taking and composing photographs and selecting the "right" photograph from which you will work. There are guidelines for using the view finder and choosing a format. There are illustrations and photographs provided as examples.

You will then discover how to turn your photograph into a black and white study to determine the values more accurately. From the value study, you will do sketches to become more comfortable and familiar with the subject matter. You then will be able to analyze the composition and easily make changes.

You'll follow the procedure of how to do an underpainting and see how useful it can be. After the underpainting is complete, you will add big shapes. The book shows you how to effectively layer the pastels and use many different kinds of strokes. The different stages of development are shown and evaluated. The instructions end with the finished painting.

Pastels offer an outlet for beauty, creativity and endless individual expression. I think you will find much enjoyment and fulfillment in this versatile medium. I hope this book will be your inspiration and take your pastel painting to new heights.

"Bend of the River II"
30" x 22"

"Lake in Scotland"
36" x 24"

TABLE OF CONTENTS

Part 1

WORKING WITH PASTELS

"Betty's Garden"
22" x 15"

PASTEL SOCIETY OF AMERICA
HISTORY OF PASTELS

Technically, Pastel is powdered pigment, rolled into round or square sticks and contained by methycellulose, a non-greasy binder. It can be blended with finger and stump, or left with visible strokes and lines. Generally, the ground is toned paper, but sanded boards and canvas are also popular. If the ground is covered completely with Pastel, the work is considered a Pastel Painting; a Pastel Sketch shows much of the ground. When protected by fixative and glass, Pastel is the most permanent of all media, for it never cracks, darkens or yellows.

Historically, its origin can be traced back to the Sixteenth Century, when Guido Reni, Jacopo Bassano, and Federigo Barocci were notable practioners. Rosalba Carriera, 1675-1750, a Venetian lady artist, was the first to make consistent use of Pastel. Chardin, 1699-1779, did portraits with a hatching stroke, while Quentin de la Tour, 1704-1788, preferred the blended, velvety finish. Thereafter, a galaxy of artists, Mengs, Nattier, Copley, Delacroix, Millet, Manet, Renoir, Toulouse-Lautrec, Redon, Vuillard, Bonnard, Glackens, Whistler and Hassam, just to list the more familiar names, used Pastel as finished work, rather than for preliminary sketches.

Degas was the most prolific user of Pastel, and its champion, for he raised it to the full brilliance of oil. His protégé, Mary Cassatt, introduced the Impressionists and Pastel to her wealthy friends in Philadelphia and Washington, and thus to the United States. Today, many of our most renowned living artists, have distinguished themselves in Pastels, and have enriched the world with this glorious medium.
Pastel Society of America, Inc.

Flora Galdini Giffuni
Pastel Society of America
Copyright © 2002

FACTS ABOUT PASTELS

There are many pastel societies throughout the world today. Pastel books and magazines have increased in numbers as the popularity of the medium grows.

Today, pastel paintings have the status of oil and watercolor as a major fine art medium.

Pastels must never be confused with colored chalk. Chalk is a limestone substance impregnated with dye.

Pastel can be combined with watercolor, gouache, acrylic, charcoal or pencil in a mixed media painting, but it is incompatible with oil paint.

MATERIAL LIST

Wallis Paper 48" x 10 yards. Professional Grade 18" x 24" or 24" x 36."
Once in a while, I split a roll with one of my friends. The rolled paper is hard to get to lay flat but it is great if you want to do some larger pieces.

NuPastels (Hard Pastels) 96-piece set. They last a long time and are excellent for underpainting. The color assortment is wonderful. I use these in the beginning of all my paintings.

Soft Pastels (Start with 60 to 80) My favorites are Schmincke and Unison. I also love the 20-piece Diane Townsend. I continue to try many others that come on the market, and often add some colors to my large assortment. I prefer the muted colors of Schmincke.

Pastel Pencils Stabilo CarbOthello set of 48, I use these for fine lines or blending.

Barrier Cream For hand protection, or use close fitting latex gloves.

Mask To avoid inhaling the powder from the Pastels.

Pastel Brush/Round Stubby Soft brush
Used to brush off pastel from some part of a painting as a means of erasing pastel from sanded paper.

Bristle Brush For underpainting

Mineral Spirits To be used with Bristle Brush to cover sanded paper with color.

Fixative Used to "fix" pastels so they do not fall from the painting.

Gator Board Have it cut one inch bigger than paper. 19" x 25" or 25" x 37".

Bankers Clips /Bulldog Clips

Easel Working vertical will allow pastel dust to fall downward.

Paper Towels Use towels to line tray of easel to catch pastel dust.

Plein Air Painting

Painting outdoors directly from nature is known as Plein Air Painting. It is not a new concept. It has been going on for many decades. In fact, it was the way artists painted landscapes before the camera was invented. Groups have formed all over the country that share the pleasure of painting from nature. These groups plan painting trips and meet together for outdoor painting. Their members believe that this is the only way to get a true "feel" for the subject matter. The reasoning is that the camera does not capture all the nuances of nature.

With Plein Air Painting, it is necessary to become disciplined and focused because with the ever changing light, you must capture what is most important, quickly.

Plein air painters argue: the camera has only one eye, and humans have two. Two eyes are better than one for viewing the landscape and getting a true perspective rather than the distorted version from the camera.

I believe students should experience painting from nature, and every effort should be made to work in this manner. I do think the experience is most important in the development of any artist.

When I travel I love to do Plein Air Painting. However, I also work from photographs, so I take many pictures in my travels. They are also useful as references.

Studio Painting

Studio Painting is what I call "Con Aire" painting—meaning with air conditioning and heating, according to the season. The convenience of just going down some steps to my well lighted, cool, bug-free studio and working from photographs has its advantages. I work every day regardless of the weather, using my full compliment of pastels or oils on my sturdy easel enjoying the sound of classical music in the background.

There is a challenge to making a painting out of a photograph. The challenge is to creatively improve the color, composition or the subject matter itself. It means you put more of yourself into the interpretation and execution of your painting.

"Lake Side"
30" x 22"

Part 2

CREATING A PASTEL PAINTING

STEP BY STEP

STEP BY STEP

I am going to take you through each step in creating a pastel painting. We will focus on working from photographs. Each step is explained and illustrated in detail.

Cameras, Viewfinders, Underpainted Sanded Paper.

1. Taking Photographs
2. Selecting Photograph for Painting
3. Using View Finder
4. Making Value Study
5. Sketching from Study
6. Underpainting
7. Showing Strokes
8. Drawing Big Shapes
9. Layering Pastels
10. Evaluating Painting

1. TAKING PHOTOGRAPHS

You don't have to be a professional photographer. You don't have to have expensive equipment. Even a throw-away camera can work. You don't have to travel great distances to gather material. You will be surprised how many "paintings" you can find in your neighborhood or in your own back yard. Taking your own photographs is important. Painting from photographs that have been published in magazines, newspapers and books is an infringement on copyright laws. It is someone else's work. Don't copy!

The best time to take photographs for landscape painting references is early in the morning or late in the afternoon when shadows are long and add interest to the composition. You can experiment with a different point of view and be creative in what you choose to photograph. When taking photographs for use as subject matter, be sure to take verticals as well as horizontals. Also include some of the surrounding trees and bushes for reference. Sometimes you need more information when you begin to work on your painting. Also, it is a good idea to take both distant shots and close-ups.

Look for good composition before taking your photos. See Part 2, "Composition" under ELEMENTS OF ART AND DESIGN.

Do you want a high horizon with little sky?
Do you want big sky and low horizon?
Can you eliminate unwanted debris?

You are in control. When I am traveling to different locations, I have no control over the time of day when I will arrive at a destination. Therefore, I have to take my photos when I can, morning, noon or night, rainy, cloudy or sunny. So I work to get the best composition I can and make notes in my journal about the location and anything special. I often make some quick sketches and make my notes directly on the sketch. This creates a permanent file and reference material for other paintings.

Even though I stress taking good photographs, sometimes my paintings are better from a bad photo because I have had to put more of myself into it while making necessary changes.

COMPOSE YOUR SHOTS

LOW HORIZON

HIGH HORIZON

LIGHT AND DARK AREAS ARE BALANCED

2. SELECTING A PHOTOGRAPH FOR A PAINTING

Not all photographs make good paintings. Knowing this will help you to be more selective in choosing your photo shots. You will develop an instinct about what makes a good photo for a painting.

Ask yourself: Is the subject matter pleasing? Do I like the subject? Can I visualize it as a painting? Is it within my capabilities? For instance, if drawing is not my strong suit, does this involve a lot of perspective or details that will be too difficult? Should I try it anyway? Don't be afraid to take these shots, but try to simplify them.

Next, make some decisions about how to approach it. Will it look better as a small intimate painting or does it need room to expand it to a grand vista?

Then consider if there is enough information. Is the subject overdone? Think about the focal point. If there is one, be sure it is not right in the middle. If there isn't a focal point, do I have to make one? Is it boring? These decisions do not have to be made at this time but it will help you take better photographs if you keep asking questions about your selection of subject material. With all these answers do you still feel an excitement or a compulsion to paint it? If you do, then go to it!

This is the photograph that was selected to take you Step by Step through making a pastel painting.

3. USING VIEW FINDER

View Finders are useful tools. I keep several with
my supplies. They help you get the most from
your photographs.

There are several types of view finders.
An opening 1 1/2" x 2" cut out of cardstock is
easy to make.
An empty 35mm slide mount is ready made.
Also, two "L" shapes can be cut from cardstock
with clips to hold them in position.
This allows for flexibility in sizing.

Use a view finder on photographs to crop and
choose the best composition.

Use it to change the format from horizontal to
vertical or to raise or lower the horizon.
See "Format" under Elements of Art and Design,
Part 3.

Take your time focusing as much as you would
when using a camera.

Try some with larger openings.

While you are focusing and viewing your photo,
try imagining how it will look as a painting.

Go with your gut feeling on your decision.

4. MAKING VALUE STUDY

I would like to point out how it helps to have a black and white study of the photograph before starting to paint. Viewing makes you "see" the subject matter without the influence of color.

The VALUE STUDY will help you judge the values more accurately. I use my copier to get a black and white copy, or a grey-scale print from my computer. I can see at a glance that there is not enough contrast. When photos are taken on a cloudy day and there is little contrast, the value study helps you decide what changes you want to make, and where you will put the emphasis. It helps you be more creative.

I often make a quick sketch from the Value Study. It is helpful to become more familiar with the subject matter. When I made the sketch, I decided the composition needed some verticals to balance the painting, so I added two trees instead of the fence. The diagonal shadows from the trees also helped to add interest and tension.

5. SKETCHING FROM STUDY

These are some quick sketches from another day that I did on location. I also take photos for reference. As you can see, I made a vertical sketch and a horizontal; I used ink. I often use pencil or charcoal. The painting shown below is from the sketches and photo.

On this painting I did not use my usual red for the underpainting. I used Wallis Belgium Mist sanded paper.

"Chadds Ford"
25" x 19"

6. UNDERPAINTING

I almost always underpaint my paper before I start a Pastel. The exceptions are when I am using a paper that already is tinted. Sometimes I am in a hurry and do not have any prepared paper. When this happens I have to work harder to layer my colors, as the underpainting already acts as a layer of color. What I like most is when I have a painting with a lot of green, the red underpainting showing through adds a real sparkle to the finished painting.

I start by covering the sanded paper with a bright red NuPastel. This is a harder, less expensive pastel that does an adequate job of covering the surface.

Then, I use a large brush and wet the entire surface blending the red pastel using mineral spirits. On Wallis paper water can be used, but takes longer to dry.

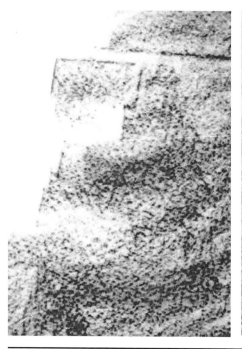  

UNDERPAINTING WITH RED

Using different colors for underpainting is fascinating. While red is the color I use most often, there are some nice surprises with experimentation. If I have a predominantly Blue subject matter, then an orange is a good choice. The underpainting that adds the most sparkle is a bright yellow. It works well even with a predominantly Green subject matter.

I also use the Wallis paper "Belgium Mist," which is a taupe color. It has a quiet, even effect.

I often prepare several sheets of paper at a time so I am ready when I want to start a painting. I prefer the brighter colors instead of white and enjoy the different effects of the colors.

Another benefit of underpainting is if you leave enough of the color showing and have not covered it up with layers of pastel, the color showing through will create a UNITY throughout your painting. This is especially helpful when a landscape has a scattering of subjects that needs something to tie them together. It works.

These sketches show the red underpainting and look very painterly.

"Chattahoochee I"   ""Chattahoochee II"   www.elsiedresch.com
8" x 10"   8" x 10"

UNDERPAINTING ON SANDED PAPER

These are some of the different colors I use on sanded paper. The taupe is "Belgium Mist" Wallis paper. The black is "Art Spectrum" and the yellow and red are those that I have underpainted using NuPastel brushed with mineral spirits.

UNDERPAINTING EXAMPLES

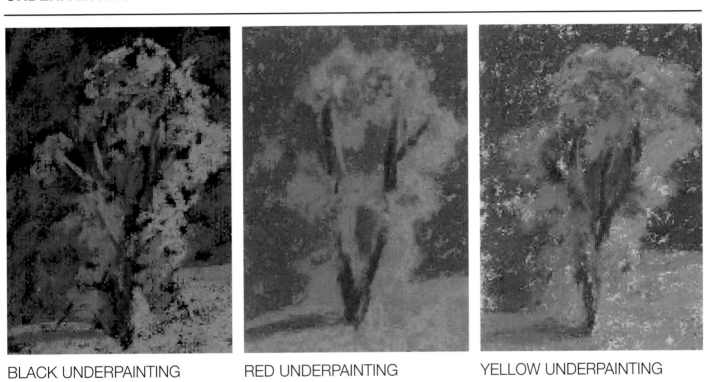

BLACK UNDERPAINTING   RED UNDERPAINTING   YELLOW UNDERPAINTING

The colors shown below were used on each of the above examples.
See how the different color underpaintings look using the same palette.

7. SHOWING STROKES

Strokes are the marks that you make to fill an area. You can produce different textures by the strokes. It is important that you practice and experiment with making marks. Start getting the feel of hard pastels versus softer ones. Then, use the side of a stick and get big broad strokes. This way you get a wide flat area. When you shorten the stroke using the flat motion you will get a different effect. Using the edge of the pastel and a tapping motion with a softer pastel will produce small dotty marks.

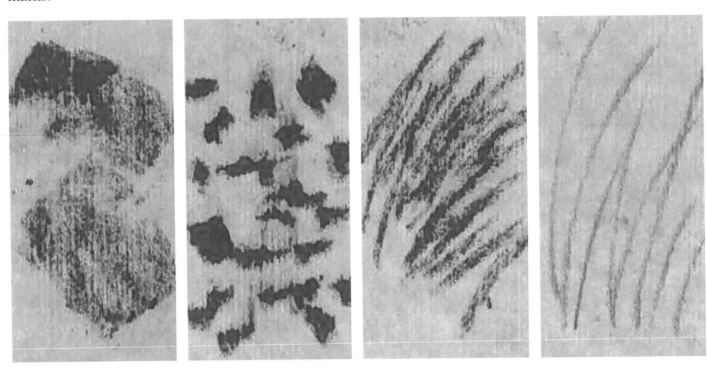

Using the tip of the pastel can give a long grassy look.

Putting different colors together using the same strokes will create a texture. See the section on "Color and Layering" under "The Elements of Art and Design."

As you work you will develop your own pattern, and after some practice, your own style will emerge.

STROKES

Try these different strokes. Add some of your own. Practice and work at it.

8. DRAWING BIG STROKES

In review,
I have gathered the photograph, the grey
scale of the photograph and the sketch.

In the sketch, in
place of the fence,
I added the two
trees in front and
smaller trees in the
background to give
some vertical
balance.

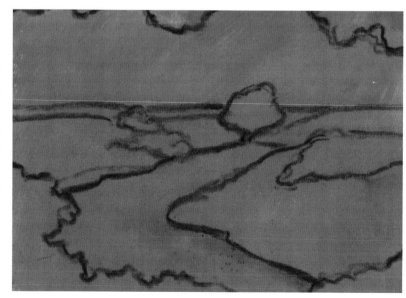

You are ready to work. On the prepared
red sanded paper draw the shapes of the
selected photograph keeping it simple.
Here, I eliminated the fence (we will add it
back later) then I opened up the solid line
of trees with more sky openings.
I used charcoal because it is easier to erase
the lines as you draw.

It will look like a coloring book.

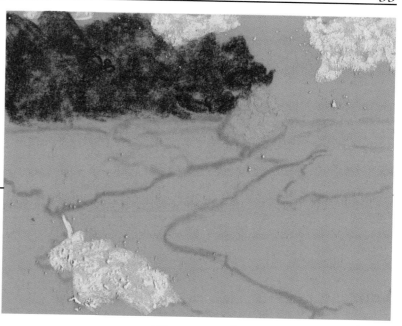

9. LAYERING PASTELS

From the charcoal drawing of big shapes, I start coloring in the these shapes with broad flat strokes using the basic colors. It should resemble a coloring book.

Then I add more colors with short strokes. I keep adding layers of pastel working over the entire surface. I vary the strokes and follow the contour of the land.

As I progress, the painting emerges. Now I step back and evaluate the painting.

I continue to add colors using the photograph as a guide. I change the water and add more color to the shapes that are still visible.

Start with big strokes

Detail of strokes

10. EVALUATING THE PAINTING

As I add the layers of color, I begin putting in the details. First, I put in the fence. I like how the dark fence adds some sparkle. I also put in the trees from my original sketch. Two trees look skimpy, so I add another. The shadows from the trees make a nice diagonal line in the foreground. Of course, I will darken the water. As I continue to study and evaluate, I still think the trees look skimpy. I will increase the size of the trees and give more weight to the foreground by adding more foliage at the bottom.

CONTINUE EVALUATING

The painting takes shape as I make a few changes in some of the colors. I think the water is too red so I darken it. Then with the darker water, the light grasses and bushes will stand out with the contrast.

The diagonal shadows could be darkened, too, and maybe some darks on the trees in the back. I will work over the entire painting adding colors and sparkle.

FINAL PAINTING

"Summer Day"
25" x 19"

Part 3

THE ELEMENTS OF

ART AND DESIGN

THE ELEMENTS OF ART AND DESIGN

The elements that are used in the language of art are LINE, SHAPE, TEXTURE, COLOR, FORM, SPACE and VALUE. A work of art is created when these elements are arranged in a manner that follows the rules or principles of art.

Knowing the elements used in the language of art is not enough. In order to create a work of art these elements must be arranged in a manner that follows the principles, or rules, of art. The basic principles of art are BALANCE, VARIETY, CONTRAST, RYTHYM, MOVEMENT, PROPORTION and UNITY.

When we went Step by Step through the process of creating a painting, we were applying knowledge of these elements and principles of art. I have simplified these definitions to keep them as concise as possible.

ELEMENTS OF ART

LINE: There are a variety of lines: Straight, curved, vertical, horizontal, diagonal, short, long, thick, thin, broken, solid and whole. A line is a path of a moving dot. Lines create boundaries and make shapes.

SHAPE : There are four basic shapes that are two dimensional: Circle, square, triangle and rectangle. These are geometric shapes. Uneven shapes, such as clouds and trees, are organic shapes. See section on Shapes.

TEXTURE: There are many different textures: rough, smooth, soft, hard, shiny, dull, fuzzy and bumpy. In a painting, different textures can be used to add variety and contrast. Texture is the way something feels or looks like it may feel.

COLOR: The three primary colors are: red, yellow, blue. By mixing a combination of these colors, secondary and tertiary colors result. The three secondary colors are: green, orange, violet. There are six tertiary colors: red-orange, yellow-orange, yellow-green, blue-green, blue-violet, red-violet. See section on Color and Color Dominance.

VALUE: Value is lightness or darkness. It is the amount of light or dark a color contains when compared to black and white. I urge everyone to make a value chart to become familiar with values. See section on Values.

FORM: Form refers to the three-dimensional quality of an object.

SPACE: The space the object occupies is called "positive" space and the area surrounding the object is called the "negative" space. These terms also apply to shapes.

PRINCIPLES OF DESIGN

Some of the principles of design are as follows: BALANCE, VARIETY, CONTRAST, UNITY, OPPOSITION, and RHYTHM.

BALANCE: Balance can be achieved by weight, size, color, space, vertically and horizontally by arranging the elements so that the visual "weight" of the different elements work together to stabilize the entire work of art.

VARIETY: Variety in shapes and shape sizes can help to make a pleasing design. Variety eliminates monotony. Variety can be achieved by alternating line widths (thick, thin) color intensities (bright, dull), values (light, dark). Variety is applied by adding or changing the different elements.

CONTRAST: Using different textures next to each other can create contrast. Warm and cool colors used together can create contrast. Different shape sizes can create contrast.

UNITY: The whole or total effect of a work that results from the right combination of harmony and variety. Similarities of shapes, color, line, and texture can create unity. This is the overall arrangement that makes all of the elements appear as one unified piece of art.

OPPOSITION: Opposition is having some tension in the forms. Vertical trees vs. horizontal land may seem quite static at times, and use of some diagonal clouds or slanting shadows can create some tension or opposition.

RHYTHM: Rhythm involves the repeating of an element to make the work seem active or alive. REPETITION can be included in this category.

COMPOSITION DEFINITION

The placement of the different objects in a painting are those design elements that lead the viewer's eye around the surface of painting through the use of shapes, line, pattern, space and/or texture in a harmonious manner. The arrangement can create a sense of motion and activity or stability and calm.

This painting was done from a photograph in North Georgia. The textured leaves on the tree lead you to look down; the repetition of little weeds leads your eye across the bottom of the painting while the light area of the water takes you back up again. There is a sense of calm and serenity here.

"Georgia October"
24" x 30"

COMPOSITION: SPACE DIVISION

The "Field of Flowers" was done from the photograph above. It was an overcast day. The house, surrounded by wildflowers, was beautiful, even on a dull day.

As you can see, I changed the horizontal photo to a vertical painting so I could focus on the flowers.

I changed the space division to do this. It makes for a more interesting painting. The photograph is devided in thirds. This can be boring.

"Field of Flowers"
22" x 30"

COMPOSITION

When Composition is being discussed, the first thing that comes to mind is "Don't ever put something important in the middle and don't divide anything in HALF. Following are my easy-to-remember guidelines about Composition.

THE THREE THREES

SMALL, MEDIUM, LARGE
This refers to space division--the size of the elements in the painting such as sky, water or trees. Making these spaces in the different sizes adds variety and interest to the composition. If the space is divided in two, then the two spaces should be different.

LIGHT, MEDIUM, DARK
Obviously, this concerns values and contrast–important elements in paintings.

FOREGROUND, MIDDLEGROUND, BACKGROUND
There should be a definite change in the stronger strokes, warmer color of the foreground compared to the smaller strokes and cooler color in the distance. The middle ground should be the transition between the two areas. Often a painting can be improved by applying this theory.

COMPOSITION: THE THREE THREES

VALUES

SPACE

DEPTH

VALUES: MEDIUM   DARK   LIGHT

SPACE: SMALL   MEDIUM   LARGE

DEPTH: FOREGROUND   MIDDLEGROUND   BACKGROUND

COMPOSITION FOCAL POINT

Not all paintings have focal points. In some subject matter a focal point might be a distraction to the mood of the painting. In a panorama, you would lose the vastness of the setting if you accented one part to create a center of interest.

Sometimes a painting will lead your eye to a place in the painting and then miss the opportunity to create a center of interest there. How often do you see a road lead you through a painting only to end up as a dark area with nothing happening?

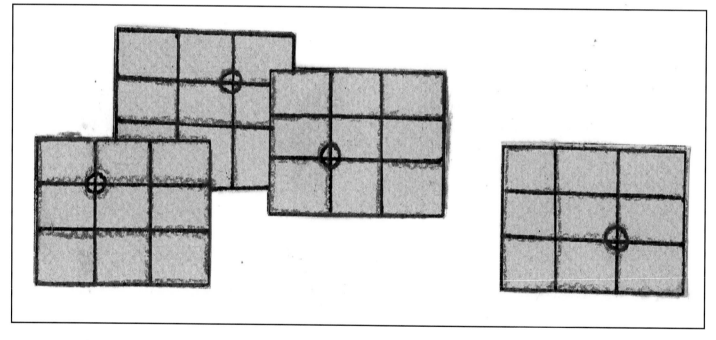

However, if early in your planning you decide on a center of interest or the photograph already shows one, it is important to place it in the right location in the painting. It also is necessary to decide if you are going to use high contrast to achieve this, or less dramatically, warm against cool, bright against dull or large against small. Whichever way you choose, the rest of the painting should remain subordinate to the focal point. One of the easiest ways to plan the placement is to draw a rectangle, then divide it in thirds like tic-tac-toe, using one of the four intersections as the location for the center of interest.

COMPOSITION FORMAT

What size and shape paper? So much of this is personal choice. So much of it has to do with the subject matter. Some of it has to do with your mood, your energy, and how you feel about the subject. Choose a large format for a delicate theme. Experiment with various sizes and shapes to find the one that suits your mood.

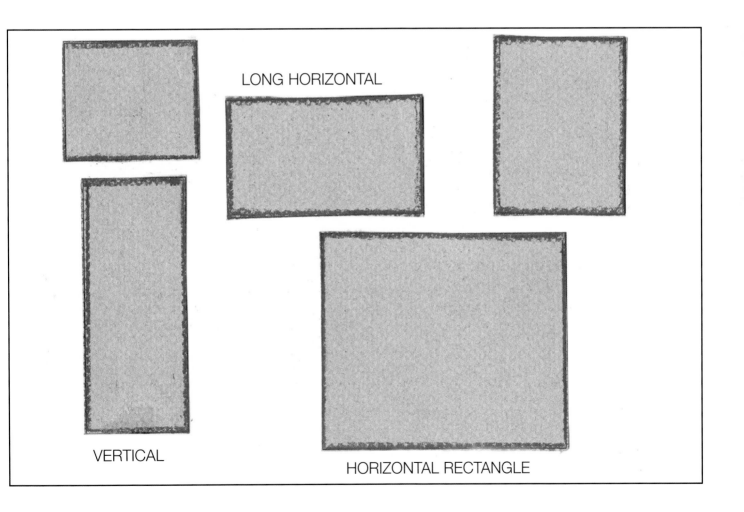

LONG HORIZONTAL

VERTICAL

HORIZONTAL RECTANGLE

COMPOSITION PITFALLS TO AVOID

When tree, buildings or people are placed in a composition, avoid putting the subject hanging on the edge of canvas or paper. Above, the point of the roof is hanging by a thread at the edge of the paper.

The solution on the upper right shows that you can crop the roof or on lower right, lower the house so that there is more sky showing above the roof, so it is no longer on the edge.

COMPOSITION PITFALLS TO AVOID

Trees point outward
Road ends in corner.

Boring- no variety
Trees meet edge of paper.

Unbalanced.

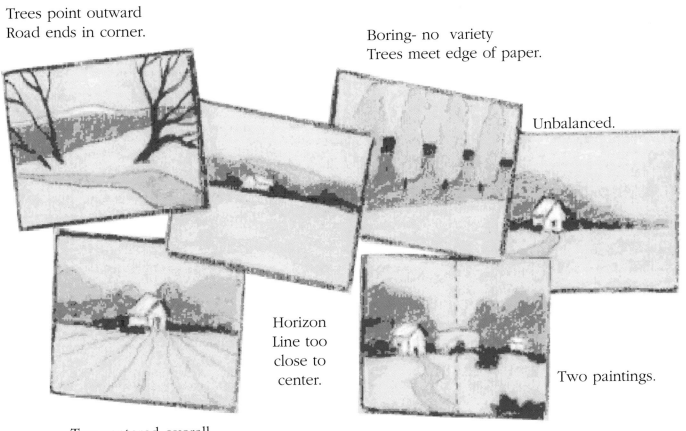

Horizon
Line too
close to
center.

Two paintings.

Too centered overall.

VALUES: SCALE

Values is the hardest concept for many students. So, first, I have every student make a Value Chart. This will help you visualize LIGHT TO DARK.

With Pastels, because you don't have to actually mix colors as they are already made in stick form, Values are a little easier to identify and choose. The manufacturers sell sets of "Darks" and "Lights." In a set of "Darks," there will be the darkest value of each color, and in a set of "Lights" the lightest value of each color.

Shown below are three sets of values: light, medium and dark. In each set, one of the squares does not fit, as the value is a little lighter or darker than the others. This is one way to learn how to read Values. This is important because you are able to translate photographs that have been done as VALUE STUDIES and make them into successful paintings. It is often said that if the Value is correct, any color will work.

Squint your eyes and you will see the square that doesn't fit.

VALUES: LOW, MEDIUM AND HIGH KEY

In a simple landscape we are looking at the three or four basic Values. The source of light (the sun) will show lightest in the sky. The next lightest value is where the light is reflected most, that is the ground and foreground. Buildings, trees or background will be the darkest.

A painting done from the lightest end of the value scale, will be considered "high key." A painting done from the darkest end of the value scale is "low key" and of course, a painting done from the middle values on the value scale will be "middle key." There will be distinct differences in the values, as each painting will have lights, mediums and darks; but COMPARED to the other paintings, they will read as fitting into one of the three categories

MIDDLE KEY

HIGH KEY

LOW KEY

COLOR

Color, or the lack of it, is what gives paintings impact and emotion. It sets a painting apart and gives it its own personality. The same subject matter and composition done with a different palette can change the mood entirely. It is often considered the most important element in a painting.

You have seen color wheels showing the primary colors (red, yellow and blue) with the secondary colors (green, orange and violet). The secondary colors are made by mixing two primary colors together. The six tertiary colors (RO, YO, YG, BG, BV, RV) are made by mixing a primary color with a secondary color.

With pastels you don't have to mix your colors because the pastels have already been mixed into individual sticks. This is why you see such a large assortment of colors in the artist's pastel boxes. A broad assortment of colors gives you a better selection from which to find the exact color and value you need for that sky, flower, building, road or grass in sunshine or in shadow. Some manufacturers have grouped boxes of lights, darks, portraits, landscapes into sets and there is even a box of 85 shades of green.

COLOR LAYERING

Mixing with pastels is actually done by layering colors and overlapping them. With several colors next to each other the eye mixes them. Colors and different values can be made richer by layering several values of the same color.

Examples below show the progression. The first illustration has just one layer of each color. The second one shows two layers of each color, while the third has several layers. These samples were done on sanded paper that was prepared with yellow underpainting color.

COLOR DOMINANCE

I once attended a workshop in which the teacher asked his students what color they wanted him to use as the dominating color.

He then demonstrated his skills and the results were amazing. He later revealed the same setting in different dominating colors. I thought it was fun!

I like using this method to get away from so many green landscapes. In the painting below, I chose warm gold colors to do this painting, removed the building and turned it into a vertical.

The dominating color made this more appealing than the photograph.

"Summer Lace"
30" x 40"

COLOR DOMINANCE

This beautiful farm was along Route 81 in Pennsylvania.   Everything was glowing this autumn day, so I named the painting "Rose Hill". I do not have the photograph.

"Rose Hill"
24" x 24"

COLOR DOMINANCE

Both paintings shown reflect color dominance. It is fun to try this using the same photograph with different palettes.

"Red December"
28" x 22"

"Pont Neuf"
22" x 19"

COLOR DOMINANCE

There was a long passenger train along the water, but I chose to eliminate it in favor of focusing on the trees.

"Field of Poppies"
30" x 22"

SHAPES: POSITIVE AND NEGATIVE

When a mark is made on paper we instantly have two shapes: the mark and the space around it. The shapes we intentionally put into the design are the "positive shapes." The rest of the surface is known as the "negative" and "incidental" shape. The negative shapes are changed when the positive shapes are changed. The drawings of the flower and the tree show the negative areas in red.

 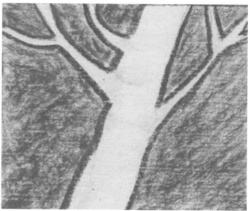

Look at the shapes around your water or the shapes surrounding your road. Are they pleasing? Look at the shape of your mountain. Is it too pointed or too rounded? Does it resemble triangles or twin peaks?

Train yourself to observe and critique your work. Look at the space between your trees. Are they too even? Can you vary the spaces and the thickness of the trees?

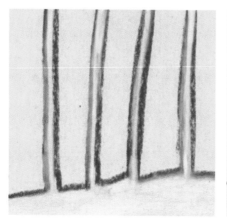 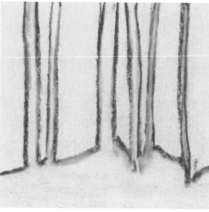

The simple drawings show how much better the varied trees look compared to the stilted, evenly spaced trees.

SHAPES

Geometric shapes such as circles, triangles or squares can be boring because they have no variation in their dimensions. If the foliage of a tree fits into a circle, for example, it will be dull. Change the shape into two different dimensions or add another shape.

Lollipop Tree fits
into circle.

Change shape adding
another circle.

If we place a triangle in one of the corners of a painting, it will be distracting in the overall view as it will draw your attention to that corner and not let you move across the painting as you should.

I suggest that instead of a sharp triangular corner, you extend the shape to form a longer side to the triangle as shown in the photograph on the right.

"Jekyll Sunrise"
28" x 22"

Part 4

WORKING IN A SERIES

WORKING IN A SERIES

Working on a series can be fun and challenging. A series usually consists of ten paintings that have something in common. It could be that they are all of the same location, or of the same subject, different locations. It also could be the same subject done at different times of the day, such as Monet's "Haystacks" or of different arrangements, as in his water lilies.

When I return from a trip with many photographs and produce paintings from these, I feel that I have "series" possibility. I don't always do a whole series, but I have fun trying.

I recently did several paintings of Jekyll Island, Ga. They were all the same size, but varied from beach with the ocean, beach with dunes, beach with fences, beach with boats, etc. What was unifying was that I kept the horizons at the same level in each. Some of these are shown in the section "About Paintings."

Here, I have included some paintings from three series that I have done. "Ryan Gainey's Garden" is one. Another is the "Swan Coach House." These are both set in the Atlanta area. The third is Monhegan Island, Maine. Several paintings from this unique island are shown throughout the book with more information about my paintings there.

WORKING IN A SERIES

Ryan Gainey's garden is charming. It is set in the old community of Decatur and continues to grow when adjoining properties become available. Ryan Gainey is well known as a garden designer and for his book, *The Well-Placed Weed.*

The garden is open to the public and is also used for special occasions. Though it is not a formal garden, some of the settings are structured. However, most of the garden features rustic gates and arches with many accessories that are used creatively to add an unusual quality to the variety of views.

RYAN GAINEY'S GARDEN

"Garden Path"
30" x 24"

RYAN GAINEY'S GARDEN

"Garden Walk"
15" x 22"

"Summer
Blooms"
15" x 22"

"Summer
Garden"
22" x 15"

RYAN GAINEY'S GARDEN

"Garden Gate"
40" x 30"

SWAN COACH HOUSE

The Swan House is a beautiful mansion in Atlanta. It is a Historical Landmark built in 1926. It has recently gone through extensive renovations. Attached to this mansion are elaborate formal gardens and a coach house, known as the Swan Coach House. I have chosen four of this series to show.

"Swan Coach House III"
15" x 22"

"Swan Coach House IV"
15" x 22"

SWAN COACH HOUSE

When working in a series, it is easy to be repetitive. The exercise of a series makes you stretch and explore to keep each painting fresh.

"Swan Coach House V"
15" x 22"

"Swan Coach House VI"
15" x 22"

MONHEGAN ISLAND

"Monhegan
Shipwreck"
14" x 11"

"Red
House"
14" x 11"

Monhegan Island is known as the "Artists' Island." These are plein air paintings I have done there. I worked on 11" x 14" sanded paper on various underpaintings.

MONHEGAN ISLAND

"Rocky Cove"
14" x 11"

"Monhegan Cottage"
14" x 11"

"Lighthouse"
14" x 11"

"Shore Road"
14" x 11"

"Maine Line"
24" x 18"

Part 5

ABOUT PAINTINGS

ABOUT PAINTINGS

CREATE DRAMA

The Red House in Monhegan is well known and is painted by many visiting artists. I chose to change the colors to a warmer palette and the flowers to a taller variety. The pink sky was the right touch.

"Red House on the Water"
40" x 30"

ABOUT PAINTINGS

FORMAT CHANGE TO VERTICAL

This cloudy spring day was not ideal picture-taking weather, but the view was charming and the distant hay bales were a perfect focal point.

In addition, the value planes–the sky, mountains, trees and ground could be seen in their proper order of values. Sky, lightest; mountains and trees, darkest; ground, medium.

"Georgia Hay Bales"
24" x 36"

ABOUT PAINTINGS

COLOR

This photograph was such a vivid green with very few other colors that it became a challenge.

First, I covered the background with several shades of yellow, yellow-orange and even some pinks. Then I put in the big shapes with dark gray-greens. I next added the trunks and blues on the water with rocks.

"Whisper of the Water"
40" x 30"

ABOUT PAINTINGS

CREATE AND COLOR

First, everything was too green. I used the view finder to focus closer to the bridge, then I grouped the ducks in the foreground with some highlights on the water For balance, I had to do something in the dark area so I added the white birds in flight.

"Central Park Bridge"
28" x 22"

www.elsiedresch.com

ABOUT PAINTINGS

FORMAT

The bright sun in Taos cast some deep shadows on the pueblo. It made an interesting composition. I did not make many changes from the photograph because I liked the way the strong diagonal shape came across the front plane. I decided to exaggerate this by making it an oblong horizontal painting, I added some growth on the right to give the area some texture. The warm palette worked.

"Taos Pueblo"
24" x 36"

ABOUT PAINTINGS

CHANGED VALUES

This building on the LBJ Ranch near San Antonio, Texas, was in deep shadows.

I changed the roof to add some color to the painting and put the flowers on the hillside to give some more texture. It was quite an improvement.

"LBJ Ranch"
40" x 30"

ABOUT PAINTINGS

COMPOSITION

The details of the tree are not shown clearly because the photograph was too dark.

I moved the tree from the center to the left and made it the focal point of the painting.

The tree was on the crest of a hill on Mount Pisgah, NC.

"The Big Tree"
30" x 24"

ABOUT PAINTINGS

COMPOSITION

While the cottage was in need of repairs, I easily "fixed" it up in the painting and worked on the gardens. I later added some pink hydrangeas in the foreground.

The painting was improved by the added color and changes in composition.

"French Cottage"
36" x 24"

www.elsiedresch.com

ABOUT PAINTINGS

BE CREATIVE
This was my mother's home in the small town of
Pennapiedimonte, Chieti, in Italy.

I was told that there have been very few changes
over the years. The addition of a bathroom was the
only major improvement.

When I did the painting I added some greenery
and color.

"Momma Mia's"
22" x 28"

ABOUT PAINTINGS

CHANGE VALUES AND COLOR

This stream running along the side of the road
formed a small cove. It was not very colorful.

I added some warm reds and lightened the road and
the trees in the background. I then added some yel-
low-greens to the bushes in the water. In the foreground, I put in some bright green foliage.

Changing the values and adding color made this a
very charming painting.

"The Cove"   www.elsiedresch.com
18 " x 24"

ABOUT PAINTINGS

VARIATION

Central Park in New York, NY is where this photo-graph was taken.

In the first painting, I followed the photograph and made it misty. To get it to look misty, I added gray to the colors and softened them. It was effective.

In the second painting I brightened the colors and made it look sunny. It is fun to try this variation on a composition that you like.

"Morning Mist"
22" x 18"

"Central Park Ducks"
22" x 18"

ABOUT PAINTINGS

CHANGE HORIZON

This is one of the many plein air paintings I did while I was in Maine. Everywhere you turn there is a spectacular view. For years, it has been a favorite place for many artists.

This painting was done from the bottom of the hill looking up at the flowers. The photograph was taken at the top of the hill but was not as interesting.

"Monhegan Hillside"
14" x 11"

ABOUT PAINTINGS

EDIT PHOTO
Mount Pisgah, NC has many beautiful areas.

I have done paintings from this photograph several times. In this painting, I added the rays of light that I had seen one morning. I made several changes from the photo so the paintings would not look the same

"Misty Morn"
40" x 30"

ABOUT PAINTINGS

COMPOSITION

Originally, the shadows shown in the photograph were in the painting. The shadows divided the foreground and looked like tracks across the whole area. When I made them smaller and carried the color along the bottom of the painting, the focus changed and improved the composition.

"Blue Georgia Waters"
36" x 24"

ABOUT PAINTINGS

ENHANCE

This was taken at a winery in Santa Barbara, CA and was dull compared to the view at the location.

As a demonstration for a class, I enhanced the color and shaped the trees. It turned out so well I had a print made.

"The Winery"
24" x 18"

ABOUT PAINTINGS

FOCAL POINT
This photograph was taken in Washington, DC on a cold rainy day. The red umbrella was placed in the right location as the focal point.

"Girl with the Red Umbrella"
22" x 18"

ABOUT PAINTINGS

SIMPLIFY

I changed very little in these paintings. The composition was great and the contrast was the way I liked it.

I did simplify some of the areas and used warmer colors.

"Peggy's Cove I"
28" x 22"

ABOUT PAINTINGS

DRAMA
This photo was taken minutes before a storm. I didn't know if it would even turn out. I took advantage of the drama and heightened the contrast with more color in the buildings.

"Taos Before the Storm"
28" x 22"

www.elsiedresch.com

ABOUT PAINTINGS

TEXTURE

The color of the grass inspired me to put some Texas bluebonnets in it. I raised the horizon line so I could form a hill.

I used the side of the pastel and scumbled several colors in a downward motion to get the grassy texture.

I then used a reference photo to put in the flowers.

"Texas Bluebonnets"
30" x 24"

ABOUT PAINTINGS

ADD COLOR
Perry's Water Garden in Franklin, NC was under heavy cloud cover. I made the sky and mountains brighter, and some greens warmer. This made the cool greens stand out and the pink lotus the focal point. The underpainting of red also helped.

"Perry's Water Garden"
16" x 20"

ABOUT PAINTINGS

CHANGE SETTING

This old truck made a wonderful painting when I surrounded it with colorful flowers.

The photo was taken in the late afternoon when shadows are longest.

"Blue Truck"
14" x 11"

ABOUT PAINTINGS

VALUE AND FORMAT
Since the photo of the garden wall in Bermuda was dark, I felt I had to change the values and add color.

I chose the horizontal setting as it would give the steps some additional room and allow more grass and foliage.

"Garden Wall"
24" x 18"

ABOUT PAINTINGS

BLACK UNDERPAINTING

The photo, taken on a November day did not have much color. The foreground fences and shadows balanced the light sunny view of the farm.

Because of the contrast, I used black underpainting and liked the effect.

"Winter Day on the Farm"
22" x 18"

ABOUT PAINTINGS

VALUES

I was doing a series on beaches when I came across this view of the gulls. I lightened the beach and added more color. I believe it could be improved by having some people in it.

"Jekyll Gulls"
30" x 22"

ABOUT PAINTINGS

CREATE

We were in Yellowstone Park and came across this quiet spot along the Snake River late one afternoon. When the photograph was taken it was almost dusk so I knew it would not be a good shot, but I loved the view. I took a few notes about the colors and how I was affected by the entire atmosphere.

I worked on this painting shortly after I returned home from the trip. Later I painted two other concepts

"Ribbon of Light"
28" x 22"

ABOUT PAINTINGS

TWO OTHER CONCEPTS

It is hard to believe these paintings all came from the same poor photograph.

It shows what can happen if you turn your imagination loose and let the colors fly.

"Ribbon of Light II"
30" x 40"

"Ribbon of Light III"
25" x 19"

ABOUT PAINTINGS

FINISHING TOUCH

The fence was the finishing touch. I put the painting on a flat surface and lightly held a plastic ruler diagonally across the painting using a sharp gray pastel pencil to draw the lines in each direction. When that was done, I formed a cross on each intersection with the pencil.

"Giverney Coop"
14" x 11"

ABOUT PAINTINGS

COLOR

Adding color and doing the wire fence was fun. I used two colored pencils, one light and one dark and drew circles touching each other.

The light circles were done in the dark areas and the dark circles in the light. It really wasn't difficult.

"Snow in the Barnyard"
14" x 11"

www.elsiedresch.com

ABOUT PAINTINGS

VIEW FINDER

This charming house in Mineral Bluff, GA always has the flag out.

I just took a corner of the house and got close in. I opened up some sky holes and balanced them with the roses.

"Home Front"
40" x 30"

ABOUT PAINTINGS

EDIT

The photograph, from North Georgia, was colorful, but I didn't want the cows at this time.

I softened the colors a little and made the bushes cooler and added sky.

I liked the results enough that I did another painting with the cows.

"Summer Bounty"
28" x 22"

ABOUT PAINTINGS

COLOR

Cape Cod was cloudy on this day.

I changed the sky and added color to the grasses and beach.

I kept it fairly simple.

"Cape Cod"
25" x 19"

ABOUT PAINTINGS

INCLUDE SURROUNDINGS

When I visited the Boston Commons there were very few people around on this cold November day. I added other people with different activities. I loved working on this painting. I titled it "The Park", as I wanted it to belong to everybody.

"The Park"
36" x 24"

www.elsiedresch.com

ABOUT PAINTINGS

LAYERING

It was a dull day when this picture was taken in Hendersonville, NC. As a demonstration in one of my workshops, I followed the photo accurately on the first day. On the second day, I added the "sunshine." I tipped the trees with golden color, added light to the roof, and then used a light, soft, peachy pastel and layered it in over the road and grasses. I changed the color of the fence and gate, too. The class loved seeing the changes.

"North Carolina Farm"
28" x 22"

ABOUT PAINTINGS

SKETCH
The Weir Farm is located in Wilton, CT. There are many paintings done from this location by well known artists because J. Alden Weir, also an artist, invited them to paint this beautiful farm.

Among the famous artists that painted there were John Twachtman, Childe Hassam, Albert Pinkerton Ryder and J. Appleton Brown.

"The Weir Farm"
14" x 11"

www.elsiedresch.com

ABOUT PAINTINGS

ADD COLOR AND BALANCE

Everything was green in these North Carolina mountains. I added some color in the sky and foreground. After the painting was finished I felt that the mass of trees on the left was too heavy. I created a ridge and opened the space to form better shapes and more light.

"Mountain Ridge"
30" x 22"

ABOUT PAINTINGS

ADD VARIETY

This photo was taken in early summer on a bright, sunny day. I changed it to fall colors and added the ducks for a focal point. Notice how I made the single leaning tree into two smaller trees and straightened them a little.

"Chastain Park Ducks"
30" x 22"

www.elsiedresch.com

ABOUT PAINTINGS

VALUE

The challenge of this painting was to change it from a low key to medium key value and still keep the contrast.

It is one of my favorite paintings and has won awards.

"Fort Federika"
20" x 16"